RECENT DEVELOPMENT IN
RICE MILL
INDUSTRY

RECENT DEVELOPMENT IN
RICE MILL
INDUSTRY

By

JATIN GARG

Worldwide Published by
Pendown Press

PENDOWN PRESS

An ISO 9001 & ISO 14001 Certified Co.

Regd. Office 2525/193, 1st Floor, Onkar Nagar-A,
Tri Nagar, Delhi-110035
Ph.: 09350849407, 09312235086
E-mail: info@pendownpress.com
Branch Office 1A/2A, 20, Hari Sadan, Ansari Road,
Daryaganj, New Delhi-110002
Ph.: 011-45794768
Website: PendownPress.com

First Edition: 2020

ISBN: 978-93-90116-30-0

All Rights Reserved

All the ideas and thoughts in this book are given by the author and he is responsible for the treatise, facts and dialogues used in this book. He is also responsible for the used pictures and the permission to use them in this book. Copyright of this book is reserved with the author. The publisher does not have any responsibility for the above-mentioned matters. No part of this publication may be reproduced, distributed, or transmitted in any form or by any means, including photocopying, recording, or other electronic or mechanical methods, without the prior written permission of the publisher and author.

Disclaimer: This book is a collection of memories of its authors, along with their viewpoints on this particular subject. We have received the content of the book from the authors. Our role is limited to just viewing the content, making it more reader friendly and ensure that it is not against the sentiments of a particular community or group of people.

If any individual, company, or organisation approaches us with the claim that some of the content of this book is their Intellectual Property Right, we cannot be held responsible, even remotely, for the duplicity of the content. It is simply because, we share a fiduciary relationship with our authors and hence we believe that it is the onus of the authors to provide us with the unique content.

Layout and Cover Designed by Pendown Graphics Team
Printed and Bound in India by Thomson Press India Ltd.

CONTENTS

ABOUT ME

My name is **Jatin Garg** and I am a commerce graduate from Delhi University. I have done my masters in Ceramic application from Cardiff Metropolitan University, United Kingdom I am the CEO of the leading Vitrified abrasives manufacturing firm based in North India, Delhi.

I am working on twin mission

First is to make WORLD CLASS whitener stone/cone for Rice Mill industry which nobody has used or seen before.

Secondly is to help in doing maximum R&D in whitening of rice by developing new sizes and products for rice mill machinery manufacturers.

1
Chapter

MARKET SYNOPSIS OF INDIA RICE MILLING MARKET

Market scenario: With growing rice milling market in India, there has been an increase in the demand of the rice milling stones across the country. In last few years there has been increase in the number of foreign players in the rice milling market as well in the country. The reason lies in the supportive policies and regulations, which promote new rice mills. Government today too offers various facilities to the new entrants in the market. This has made market for the rice milling machinery manufacturers flourishing.

Furthermore, the food habit of the country is such that rice is one of the most sought-after food grains in the country & worldwide. So, quite naturally it assumes paramount importance in agriculture. Climatic conditions too are conducive for its cultivation. The monsoon and the terrain across the regions of north India, east India and south India support the rice cultivation of various grades and qualities.

The Indian Rice Milling market is expected to reach market size of USD 392.6 million by 2022. It is expected to grow at 3.51% CAGR (Compound annual growth rate) during the forecast period.

2
Chapter

RICE MILLING

Rice milling is the process of removing the husk and bran layer to produce white rice. This process can be undertaken as:

- One-step milling process where the husk and bran are removed in one pass and rice is produced directly from paddy.

- Two-step milling process where husk and the bran are removed separately and brown rice is produced as an intermediate product.

- Multi-stage milling process where rice is produced through a number of different operations and machines from paddy to white rice.

Whitening or Polishing Process

This process is part of multistage milling process. In this process, bran layer is removed from the kernel by applying friction to the grains against an abrasive surface. The total amount of bran removed is normally between 8-10% of the total rice weight. This can vary according to the variety and degree of whiteness required.

Just around 2-3 decades ago, the majority of people were doing whitening of rice by cone which were made manually by LOCAL MISTRI. This concept had numerous challenges including:

1) Huge broken % of rice.

2) Very very inconsistent polish of rice.

3) Dependency on MISTRI or FOREMAN for the manual EXPERTISE.

4) Low output of rice.

Then came the whitener stone concept in which the stones were made by using the same SILICON CARBIDE grains (Used by MISTRI) but made by VITRIFIED BOND TECHNOLOGY in which SiC grains are mixed with particular bond , pressed in hydraulic press (to give it that particular shape) & then fired in KILN/FURNANCE at 1260 C (Also known as Glass technology) and then finishing is done on CNC automatic machines to give it exact size in terms of ID (Inner diameter), OD (Outer diameter), RBS (Recess on both sides) and height (in mm).

The best part of this technology is that this gives:

1. Higher productivity.

2. Consistent polish (Same KETT) of rice

3. Consistently low broken (Non Variable) of rice.

And then one more EXCELLENT development was made particularly for Golden Sella (Par Boiled) Rice. The problem with the Sella (Par Boiled) Rice is that polish or bran is stuck on rice as if it is being GLUED to it by means of adhesive and hence it is very difficult to remove the polish or bran present on the rice. Then came READYMADE CONE technology and in this technology, the concept and technology of CONE was used but after removing the demerits linked to it. These demerits were removed by making cones with same VITRIFIED BOND TECHNOLOGY where cones were made in hydraulic presses and heated in KILN/FURNANCE at 1300° C for 7 days. This gave very good polish of rice in Sella (Par Boiled) Rice but with a far less broken percentage of rice.

In this process, the grain is whitened by the abrasive action of rice kernel passing between moving whitener stone and stationary screen.

3

Chapter

ROLL OF OUR NEW DEVELOPED WHITENER STONE IN REDUCING BROKEN % OF KERNELS

The whitening process applies pressure to the grain, which generates heat which causes cracking, breakage of some kernels. We have developed a new whitener stone which gives long lasting free cutting behavior which helps in reducing heat generation and thereby reduction in broken%. We call this SELF DRESSING BOND TECHNOLOGY STONES 2.0.

After use for some days the edge of grains become BLUNT and the stone eventually is unable to polish the rice to the same amount as it is expected to. To overcome this problem, the operator has to DRESS the wheels and this allows new fresh layer of grains to come on the surface and the wheel starts functioning normally again. Our R&D team worked extensively and tirelessly for many years and finally we have come up with THE BOND which is better known as SELF DRESSING BOND 2.0. The USP of this bond is that whenever the top layer of stone gets BLUNT, instead of grinding, it starts to produce friction. Our SELF DRESSING BOND 2.0 lets go the blunt layer of grain and allows fresh conical grain layer to SURFACE and do the polishing of rice.

4

Chapter

SPECIAL FEATURES OF NEWLY DESIGNED SELF DRESSING BOND TECHNOLOGY WHITENER STONE 2.0

- Reduction in broken rice%
- More whiteness due to fine finish in rice
- More yield per ton of paddy processing
- Better rice quality

5
Chapter

STANDARD COMPANY FOR THE NON STANDARD WHEELS

Our company is better known as STANDARD COMPANY FOR THE NON STANDARD WHEELS in the AUTOMOBILE and BEARING industry. This name we have earned by giving fast service to machinery manufacturers and motivate them to develop new and latest machines with NEW sizes of wheels being used in them which in turn helps industry end users to make better product and increase productivity.

Same principle we have applied to RICE industry as well and have been giving service and support to rice mill machinery manufacturers to develop more productive Whitening machines which give better polish of rice and are able to reduce costs by saving on broken percentage of rice and increase productivity.

6

Chapter

OUR SUCCESS STORY

**A CASE STUDY OF RICE MILL OWNER WORRIED
ABOUT REJECTION OF SAMPLE OF RICE**

We had been supplying rice rubber rolls to one of our customers in Secunderabad, UTTARPRADESH. Though we had been supplying rolls to them and had discussed with them about our product WHITENER STONE, but they were interested to buy their stone VTA 15 from SATAKE company itself.

One fine day in 2017, on our regular visit of our company's senior sales manager Mr Pawan Jain, found a very worried staff and owners of the mill. Upon inquiring, he got to know that their Rice samples were being rejected by some big Rice exporters' houses because some of their rice was having BRAN layer on them. Just then Mr Pawan told them about our SELF

DRESSING BOND TECHNOLOGY WHITENER STONE 2.0 and its benefits.

Next day, I went to their plant along with Mr Pawan Jain and gave detailed explanation of our product. We got the orders for three sets and I feel PROUD to say that they were able to retain all the customers who were on the brink of abandoning them and in fact they were able to deliver more than what they had promised as their Rice had more whiteness than what customer had asked for. Now they have multiplied their business and diversified also and have given us many more customers because ONE SATISFIED CUSTOMER BRINGS MANY MORE WITH HIM/HER.

www.ingramcontent.com/pod-product-compliance
Lightning Source LLC
LaVergne TN
LVHW022057190726
843495LV00014B/1796